Copyright © 2023 by Herman Strange (Author)

All rights reserved. This book or any portion thereof may not be reproduced or used in any manner whatsoever without the express written permission of the publisher except for the use of brief quotations in a book review.

This book is copyright protected. This is only for personal use. You cannot amend, distributor, sell, use, quote or paraphrase any part or the content within this book without the consent of the author. Please note the information contained within this document is for educational and entertainment purposes only. Every attempt has been made to provide accurate, up to date and reliable complete information. No warranties of any kind are expressed or implied.

Readers acknowledge that the author is not engaging in the rendering of legal, financial, medical or professional advice. The content of this book has been derived from various sources. Please consult a licensed professional before attempting any techniques outlined in this book.

By reading this document, the readers agree that under no circumstances are the author responsible for any losses, direct or indirect, which are incurred as a result of the use of information contained within this document, including but not limited to errors, omissions or inaccuracies.

Thank you very much for reading this book.

The Future of AI-Driven Crypto Investing
Subtitle: Advanced Strategies for Building and Deploying AI Trading Systems

Series: Rise of Cognitive Computing: AI Evolution from Origins to Adoption
Author: Herman Strange

Table of Contents

Introduction **6**

The current state of AI-driven crypto investing and how it has evolved since the publication of the previous book in the series 6

An overview of the topics covered in this book and how they build on the previous books in the series 8

Chapter 1: Algorithmic Trading Strategies **11**

An in-depth exploration of algorithmic trading strategies and their applications in the cryptocurrency market 11

Statistical arbitrage strategies and pairs trading 14

Mean reversion and momentum strategies 16

How to develop, test and refine algorithmic trading strategies using AI 18

Chapter 2: Reinforcement Learning for Crypto Investing **21**

An introduction to reinforcement learning and its applications in the cryptocurrency market 21

How to build and train a reinforcement learning agent for cryptocurrency trading 23

Challenges and limitations of reinforcement learning for crypto investing 25

Chapter 3: Predictive Modeling for Cryptocurrency Prices **28**

An overview of the different types of predictive models used in cryptocurrency price forecasting 28
Time series forecasting models and their applications in the cryptocurrency market 31
Using deep learning models such as recurrent neural networks (RNNs) and long short-term memory (LSTM) networks for price prediction 35
Challenges and limitations of predictive modeling for crypto investing 37

Chapter 4: Risk Management and Portfolio Optimization 39

The importance of risk management in crypto investing 39
How to use AI to optimize portfolio allocations and manage risk 42
Using value at risk (VaR) and other risk metrics to measure and manage portfolio risk 45
How to incorporate alternative data sources into risk management and portfolio optimization strategies 48

Chapter 5: Applying AI to Cryptocurrency Mining 52

An overview of cryptocurrency mining and how it works 52
How AI is being used to optimize mining operations and improve mining efficiency 54

Challenges and limitations of AI in cryptocurrency mining 57

Chapter 6: Building Your Own AI-Driven Crypto Trading System 60

A step-by-step guide to building your own AI-driven crypto trading system 60

How to choose the right AI tools and technologies for your trading system 64

Tips and best practices for building and deploying an effective AI-driven trading system 67

Conclusion 70

Recap of the key insights and takeaways from the book 70

The future of AI-driven crypto investing and how to stay ahead of the curve... 73

Advice for readers who are interested in exploring AI-driven crypto investing further........................... 76

Glossary 79
Potential References... 82

Introduction

The current state of AI-driven crypto investing and how it has evolved since the publication of the previous book in the series

The use of artificial intelligence (AI) in the world of cryptocurrency has been rapidly evolving over the past few years. In this book, we will explore advanced strategies for building and deploying AI trading systems for crypto investing. But before diving into these strategies, it is important to understand the current state of AI-driven crypto investing and how it has evolved since the publication of the previous book in the series.

The previous book in the series, "AI-Driven Crypto Investing: Strategies and Techniques for Successful Trading," provided an introduction to the world of AI-driven crypto investing. It covered the basics of machine learning and how it can be applied to the cryptocurrency market. It also provided an overview of different trading strategies, such as trend following, mean reversion, and sentiment analysis.

Since the publication of the previous book, there have been significant developments in the world of AI-driven crypto investing. One major development has been the growth of algorithmic trading in the cryptocurrency market.

Algorithmic trading involves using computer programs to automatically execute trades based on pre-defined criteria. It has become increasingly popular in the cryptocurrency market due to the high volatility and 24/7 nature of the market.

Another major development has been the use of deep learning models, such as recurrent neural networks (RNNs) and long short-term memory (LSTM) networks, for predicting cryptocurrency prices. These models have shown promising results in predicting price movements and have become an important tool for traders and investors.

In addition to these developments, there has been a growing focus on risk management and portfolio optimization in the world of AI-driven crypto investing. With the high volatility of the cryptocurrency market, it is important to manage risk and optimize portfolio allocations to maximize returns.

Overall, the use of AI in the cryptocurrency market has become more widespread and sophisticated since the publication of the previous book in the series. In this book, we will explore advanced strategies and techniques for building and deploying AI trading systems for crypto investing, taking into account these developments and the current state of the industry.

An overview of the topics covered in this book and how they build on the previous books in the series

In this book, we will explore the use of AI-driven trading systems in the context of cryptocurrency investing. Specifically, we will cover advanced strategies for building and deploying AI trading systems in the cryptocurrency market. This book builds on the previous books in the series by focusing specifically on the use of AI in cryptocurrency trading, and by providing more in-depth coverage of the latest tools, techniques, and best practices for using AI to inform trading decisions.

Chapter 1 will cover algorithmic trading strategies, including statistical arbitrage, mean reversion, and momentum strategies. We will explore how these strategies can be used in the cryptocurrency market, and how to develop, test, and refine them using AI.

Chapter 2 will focus on reinforcement learning, a subfield of machine learning that is particularly well-suited to trading systems. We will cover the basics of reinforcement learning and how it can be applied to cryptocurrency trading, including how to build and train a reinforcement learning agent for trading.

Chapter 3 will cover predictive modeling, another important area of AI for trading systems. We will explore different types of predictive models used in cryptocurrency price forecasting, including time series forecasting models and deep learning models such as recurrent neural networks (RNNs) and long short-term memory (LSTM) networks.

Chapter 4 will cover risk management and portfolio optimization, two critical areas of focus for any investor. We will explore how AI can be used to optimize portfolio allocations and manage risk, and how to incorporate alternative data sources into risk management and portfolio optimization strategies.

Chapter 5 will cover the use of AI in cryptocurrency mining. We will explore how AI can be used to optimize mining operations and improve mining efficiency, as well as the challenges and limitations of AI in cryptocurrency mining.

Finally, Chapter 6 will provide a step-by-step guide to building your own AI-driven trading system for cryptocurrency investing. We will cover how to choose the right AI tools and technologies for your trading system, and provide tips and best practices for building and deploying an effective AI-driven trading system.

By the end of this book, readers will have a solid understanding of the latest tools and techniques for using AI to inform cryptocurrency trading decisions, and will be able to build and deploy their own AI-driven trading systems with confidence.

Chapter 1: Algorithmic Trading Strategies
An in-depth exploration of algorithmic trading strategies and their applications in the cryptocurrency market

Algorithmic trading strategies are increasingly being used in the cryptocurrency market due to the fast-paced and volatile nature of the market. These strategies rely on complex mathematical algorithms that analyze market data and make trading decisions based on predefined rules.

One of the most common algorithmic trading strategies in the cryptocurrency market is statistical arbitrage. This strategy involves identifying pairs of cryptocurrencies that are correlated and taking advantage of temporary deviations in their prices. For example, if two cryptocurrencies have historically moved in the same direction but one suddenly drops in price while the other stays stable, an algorithmic trader can buy the cheaper one and sell the more expensive one, expecting that they will eventually return to their historical correlation.

Another popular algorithmic trading strategy is mean reversion. This strategy involves identifying assets that are trading at prices significantly different from their historical averages and taking a position in the opposite direction. For example, if a cryptocurrency has historically traded in a range of $50 to $100 and is currently trading at $150, an algorithmic trader using the mean reversion strategy would sell the asset, expecting that it will eventually return to its historical range.

Momentum trading is another algorithmic strategy that is commonly used in the cryptocurrency market. This strategy involves identifying assets that are experiencing significant price movements and taking a position in the same direction as the trend. For example, if a cryptocurrency has been increasing in price for several days in a row, an algorithmic trader using the momentum strategy would buy the asset, expecting that the trend will continue.

Algorithmic trading strategies can be developed and tested using artificial intelligence techniques such as machine learning. By feeding large amounts of historical data into machine learning algorithms, traders can train their algorithms to identify patterns in the data and make more accurate predictions about future price movements.

However, algorithmic trading is not without risks. One of the major risks is overfitting, which occurs when an algorithm is trained too closely to historical data and fails to perform well in new market conditions. Additionally, algorithmic trading can be impacted by sudden and unexpected events, such as regulatory changes or news events, that can cause significant price movements in the market. Traders must constantly monitor their algorithms and make adjustments to ensure they remain effective in changing market conditions.

Statistical arbitrage strategies and pairs trading

Statistical arbitrage and pairs trading are popular algorithmic trading strategies that can be applied to the cryptocurrency market.

Statistical arbitrage is a strategy that seeks to exploit the price inefficiencies of assets by taking advantage of the statistical relationships between them. In this strategy, two or more assets with a high correlation are identified, and a long position is taken on the undervalued asset while a short position is taken on the overvalued asset. This strategy is based on the assumption that the prices of two correlated assets will eventually converge.

Pairs trading, on the other hand, is a strategy that involves taking a long position on one asset and a short position on another asset that is highly correlated. This strategy involves buying an undervalued asset and selling an overvalued asset simultaneously. Pairs trading is based on the assumption that the prices of two highly correlated assets will eventually move towards their long-term mean.

In the cryptocurrency market, statistical arbitrage and pairs trading can be applied to pairs of cryptocurrencies with a high correlation. For example, Bitcoin and Ethereum are highly correlated, so statistical arbitrage and pairs trading can be applied to these two cryptocurrencies. By taking a long position on the undervalued asset and a short position on the overvalued asset, traders can profit from the price inefficiencies in the market.

However, it is important to note that statistical arbitrage and pairs trading strategies require a high degree of accuracy in identifying the correlations between assets, as well as a robust risk management system to mitigate potential losses. Additionally, these strategies are highly dependent on market conditions and may not work well in all market environments.

In conclusion, statistical arbitrage and pairs trading are powerful algorithmic trading strategies that can be applied to the cryptocurrency market. By identifying pairs of highly correlated assets and taking advantage of the price inefficiencies, traders can potentially generate profits. However, these strategies require careful consideration of market conditions and risk management practices to be successful.

Mean reversion and momentum strategies

Mean reversion and momentum strategies are two popular algorithmic trading strategies used in the cryptocurrency market. These strategies rely on different market phenomena and can be used separately or in combination to generate profitable trades.

Mean reversion trading is based on the idea that prices tend to revert to their average or mean value over time. In other words, if a cryptocurrency's price has been trending significantly above or below its mean, it is likely to eventually return to its average value. Mean reversion strategies involve identifying these deviations from the mean and taking positions that bet on the price returning to its mean.

One common mean reversion strategy is called the "pair trading" strategy. This involves identifying two cryptocurrencies that are highly correlated and trading the spread between them. The spread is the difference between the two cryptocurrency prices, and when it deviates significantly from its mean, the trader can take a position that bets on it reverting back to its mean.

Momentum trading, on the other hand, is based on the idea that prices tend to continue in the direction of their trend. If a cryptocurrency's price is increasing rapidly, it is likely to continue increasing for a period of time before eventually reversing. Momentum strategies involve identifying these trends and taking positions that bet on the trend continuing.

One popular momentum strategy is called "trend following." This involves identifying a cryptocurrency that is experiencing a strong upward or downward trend and taking a position that bets on the trend continuing. Trend following strategies can be risky, as trends can reverse suddenly, but they can also be highly profitable if the trend continues for an extended period of time.

In summary, mean reversion and momentum strategies are two popular algorithmic trading strategies used in the cryptocurrency market. Mean reversion strategies involve identifying deviations from the mean and taking positions that bet on the price returning to its mean, while momentum strategies involve identifying trends and taking positions that bet on the trend continuing. These strategies can be used separately or in combination to generate profitable trades in the volatile cryptocurrency market.

How to develop, test and refine algorithmic trading strategies using AI

Developing, testing, and refining algorithmic trading strategies using AI requires a structured and iterative approach. Here are the key steps:

1. Define your trading objective: Before you start building your trading strategy, you need to define your trading objective. This could be anything from maximizing profit to minimizing risk or achieving a specific target return. Your trading objective will guide the design of your trading strategy.

2. Collect and preprocess data: The next step is to collect data on the cryptocurrency market and preprocess it to make it suitable for use in your trading model. This includes cleaning and organizing the data, dealing with missing values and outliers, and normalizing the data to make it comparable across different time periods.

3. Feature engineering: Once your data is preprocessed, the next step is to create features that your algorithmic trading model can use to make decisions. These features could include technical indicators, such as moving averages or Bollinger Bands, or fundamental data, such as news sentiment or trading volume. Feature engineering is a

crucial step in developing an effective algorithmic trading strategy.

4. Choose an AI model: There are several AI models that can be used for algorithmic trading, including decision trees, random forests, and neural networks. The choice of model depends on your trading objective, the size of your dataset, and the complexity of your trading strategy. Deep learning models, such as convolutional neural networks (CNNs) or recurrent neural networks (RNNs), have been shown to be particularly effective in cryptocurrency trading.

5. Train and validate your model: Once you have selected an AI model, you need to train it on historical data and validate its performance using out-of-sample data. This involves splitting your dataset into training and testing sets, selecting appropriate performance metrics, and optimizing your model hyperparameters to improve its performance.

6. Backtesting: Once you have developed and validated your trading strategy, you need to test it on historical data to evaluate its effectiveness. Backtesting involves simulating trades based on your trading strategy and calculating key performance metrics, such as returns, Sharpe ratio, and drawdown. Backtesting allows you to assess the performance of your trading strategy in different market conditions and identify areas for improvement.

7. Live trading: Once you are satisfied with the performance of your algorithmic trading strategy, you can start live trading using a cryptocurrency exchange API. It is important to monitor your trading strategy regularly and make adjustments as necessary to ensure that it continues to perform effectively.

In summary, developing, testing, and refining algorithmic trading strategies using AI is a complex and iterative process that requires careful planning, data preprocessing, feature engineering, model selection, and testing. However, with the right approach and tools, it is possible to build highly effective trading strategies that can outperform human traders in the cryptocurrency market.

Chapter 2: Reinforcement Learning for Crypto Investing

An introduction to reinforcement learning and its applications in the cryptocurrency market

Reinforcement learning (RL) is a subfield of machine learning that focuses on developing algorithms that learn to make decisions based on feedback received from their environment. In the context of crypto investing, RL algorithms can learn to make trading decisions based on the current state of the market and historical data.

RL algorithms operate through a process of trial and error. They learn by receiving feedback from the environment in the form of rewards or penalties based on their actions. The goal of an RL algorithm is to learn a policy that maximizes the cumulative reward received over time.

One of the advantages of RL algorithms in crypto investing is their ability to learn from experience. By continuously interacting with the market and receiving feedback, RL algorithms can adapt to changing market conditions and improve their decision-making over time.

RL algorithms can be used for a variety of tasks in crypto investing, including price prediction, risk management, and portfolio optimization. For example, an RL algorithm can learn to predict the price of a cryptocurrency based on historical data, or it can learn to optimize a portfolio allocation based on the current state of the market.

However, RL algorithms also come with certain limitations and challenges. One challenge is the issue of data scarcity, as RL algorithms require large amounts of data to learn effectively. Another challenge is the issue of overfitting, where an RL algorithm may learn to perform well on historical data but fails to generalize to new data.

Overall, RL algorithms have shown promise in the field of crypto investing, and their potential for learning from experience and adapting to changing market conditions makes them a valuable tool for traders and investors alike. In the following chapters, we will explore how to build and train RL agents for cryptocurrency trading, as well as the challenges and limitations of using RL in this context.

How to build and train a reinforcement learning agent for cryptocurrency trading

Reinforcement learning is a type of machine learning that involves training an agent to make decisions based on feedback received from its environment. In the context of cryptocurrency trading, reinforcement learning can be used to build agents that make trading decisions based on real-time market data. Here are the steps involved in building and training a reinforcement learning agent for cryptocurrency trading:

1. Define the problem: The first step in building a reinforcement learning agent for cryptocurrency trading is to define the problem you want the agent to solve. This involves defining the trading environment, the objective of the agent, and the actions it can take.

2. Collect data: Once you have defined the problem, you need to collect data to train the agent. This involves collecting historical market data and creating a simulation environment where the agent can learn from its actions.

3. Preprocess data: The next step is to preprocess the data to make it suitable for the reinforcement learning algorithm. This involves normalizing the data, selecting relevant features, and preparing the data for use in the algorithm.

4. Train the agent: Once the data has been preprocessed, you can train the reinforcement learning agent using techniques such as Q-learning or policy gradient methods. During training, the agent learns to make decisions based on its environment and receives feedback in the form of rewards or penalties.

5. Evaluate the agent: After the agent has been trained, you need to evaluate its performance on a test dataset. This involves running the agent in a simulation environment and measuring its performance against a set of evaluation metrics.

6. Refine the agent: Based on the evaluation results, you can refine the agent and retrain it using additional data or a different set of parameters. This process is repeated until the agent achieves satisfactory performance.

Overall, building and training a reinforcement learning agent for cryptocurrency trading can be a challenging task, but it has the potential to generate significant returns if done correctly. By following these steps and continuously refining the agent, you can create a powerful tool for trading in the cryptocurrency market.

Challenges and limitations of reinforcement learning for crypto investing

Reinforcement learning is a powerful technique for training agents to make optimal decisions in complex environments. However, like any machine learning approach, it has its own set of challenges and limitations when it comes to crypto investing.

One of the biggest challenges of reinforcement learning in this domain is the high volatility and unpredictability of cryptocurrency prices. The market can be influenced by a variety of factors, such as news events, regulatory changes, and investor sentiment, which can lead to sudden and unexpected price swings. This can make it difficult for a reinforcement learning agent to learn and adapt to the changing market conditions.

Another challenge is the lack of reliable historical data for training and testing the agent. While there are many sources of cryptocurrency price data, they may not always be consistent or accurate, and they may not provide a complete picture of the market. This can make it difficult to train a reinforcement learning agent to make accurate predictions and decisions.

In addition, reinforcement learning agents require a lot of computational resources to train and optimize, which can be expensive and time-consuming. This can be a barrier for individual investors or small investment firms who may not have access to the necessary hardware or cloud computing resources.

Finally, there is the risk of overfitting or underfitting the model. Reinforcement learning agents can be prone to overfitting if they are trained on a limited amount of data or if the data is not representative of the broader market. On the other hand, underfitting can occur if the model is not complex enough to capture the nuances of the market.

Despite these challenges, there are several strategies that can be used to mitigate these issues and improve the performance of a reinforcement learning agent. These include:

1. Data preprocessing: To improve the quality of the data used for training, it can be preprocessed to remove noise, fill gaps, and correct errors. This can help to reduce the impact of unreliable data on the agent's performance.

2. Feature engineering: By selecting relevant features and transforming them appropriately, the agent can be trained on a more informative and representative set of data. This can improve the accuracy of the agent's predictions and decisions.

3. Regularization: To prevent overfitting, regularization techniques such as dropout, weight decay, or early stopping can be used to constrain the complexity of the model and encourage generalization.

4. Model selection: By selecting the most appropriate reinforcement learning algorithm and tuning its hyperparameters, the performance of the agent can be optimized. This requires careful experimentation and testing to find the best combination of settings.

In conclusion, while reinforcement learning has its own set of challenges and limitations when it comes to crypto investing, it is a powerful approach that can be used to build intelligent trading agents. By carefully selecting and preprocessing the data, engineering informative features, and tuning the model's parameters, it is possible to create agents that can learn to make profitable decisions in this complex and dynamic market.

Chapter 3: Predictive Modeling for Cryptocurrency Prices

An overview of the different types of predictive models used in cryptocurrency price forecasting

Predictive modeling is a popular approach used in the cryptocurrency market to forecast future price movements. These models use various techniques to analyze historical data, identify trends, and make predictions about future price movements. In this chapter, we will explore the different types of predictive models used in cryptocurrency price forecasting.

1. Time Series Analysis: Time series analysis is a popular approach to modeling cryptocurrency prices. It involves analyzing past price data and identifying patterns and trends in the data. Time series models use these patterns to make predictions about future price movements. Common time series models include Autoregressive Integrated Moving Average (ARIMA) models and Exponential Smoothing models.

2. Machine Learning Models: Machine learning is a subset of artificial intelligence that uses statistical techniques to enable machines to learn from data. Machine learning models can be trained to recognize patterns in data and make predictions about future price movements. Some

popular machine learning models used in cryptocurrency price forecasting include Random Forest, Gradient Boosting, and Support Vector Machines.

3. Deep Learning Models: Deep learning is a subset of machine learning that uses neural networks to recognize patterns in data. Deep learning models are capable of processing large amounts of data and identifying complex patterns that may not be easily recognizable by other models. Some popular deep learning models used in cryptocurrency price forecasting include Long Short-Term Memory (LSTM) networks and Convolutional Neural Networks (CNNs).

4. Bayesian Models: Bayesian models are a type of statistical model that uses Bayes' theorem to make predictions. Bayesian models are particularly useful for cryptocurrency price forecasting because they can incorporate new information and adjust their predictions accordingly. Some popular Bayesian models used in cryptocurrency price forecasting include Bayesian Neural Networks and Bayesian Structural Time Series models.

5. Ensemble Models: Ensemble models are models that combine the predictions of multiple models to produce a more accurate prediction. Ensemble models are particularly useful when individual models have weaknesses or make inaccurate predictions. Popular ensemble models used in

cryptocurrency price forecasting include Random Forest, Gradient Boosting, and Stacked Generalization.

6. Other Models: In addition to the models mentioned above, there are several other models used in cryptocurrency price forecasting. These include Markov Chain Monte Carlo models, GARCH models, and Hidden Markov models.

In conclusion, there are several different types of predictive models used in cryptocurrency price forecasting, each with their strengths and weaknesses. It is important to carefully evaluate the performance of these models and choose the one that is best suited to your needs. In the next section, we will discuss the process of building and testing predictive models for cryptocurrency price forecasting.

Time series forecasting models and their applications in the cryptocurrency market

Time series forecasting models are a popular choice in the cryptocurrency market due to their ability to analyze and predict trends over time. These models can be used to forecast future prices based on historical data, as well as to identify patterns and relationships between variables that may impact price movements. In this section, we will discuss some of the most commonly used time series forecasting models in the context of cryptocurrency investing.

1. Moving Average Models Moving average (MA) models are simple yet effective models that can be used to forecast future prices by analyzing past averages of a given time series. In this model, the future price is predicted based on the average of the past prices, with more recent prices weighted more heavily. One of the main advantages of MA models is their simplicity, as they only require historical price data to make predictions. However, they may not be as accurate as more complex models, as they do not take into account other factors that may impact price movements.

2. Autoregressive Models Autoregressive (AR) models are another popular choice in cryptocurrency price forecasting. These models are based on the assumption that future prices can be predicted based on past prices and their

associated errors. In an AR model, the future price is predicted based on a linear combination of the past prices and their associated errors. The order of the model refers to the number of past prices used in the prediction. AR models are particularly effective for identifying trends and patterns in price movements.

3. Autoregressive Integrated Moving Average Models Autoregressive Integrated Moving Average (ARIMA) models are a more complex version of AR models that also take into account the integrated or differenced time series. ARIMA models are particularly useful for predicting non-stationary time series data, where the mean and variance of the data change over time. In an ARIMA model, the future price is predicted based on a combination of past prices, their associated errors, and the integrated or differenced time series.

4. Prophet Models Prophet models are a relatively new type of time series forecasting model that have gained popularity in the cryptocurrency market due to their ability to account for seasonality, trends, and other external factors that may impact price movements. Prophet models are based on the decomposition of the time series into trend, seasonality, and error components, and use a Bayesian framework to generate probabilistic forecasts. Prophet

models are particularly effective for predicting long-term trends and patterns in price movements.

5. Recurrent Neural Network Models Recurrent neural network (RNN) models are a type of deep learning model that can be used for time series forecasting in the cryptocurrency market. RNN models are particularly effective for predicting non-linear relationships and patterns in time series data. These models work by processing input data through a sequence of hidden layers that allow the network to retain information about past observations. RNN models can be trained to predict future prices based on historical price data, as well as to identify patterns and relationships between variables that may impact price movements.

In conclusion, time series forecasting models are a powerful tool for predicting future price movements in the cryptocurrency market. By using historical data to identify patterns and relationships between variables, these models can provide investors with valuable insights into market trends and help them make informed investment decisions. However, it is important to remember that no model is perfect, and that other factors such as market sentiment, news events, and regulatory changes may also impact price movements. Therefore, investors should use a combination of different models and strategies to optimize their returns and minimize their risks.

Using deep learning models such as recurrent neural networks (RNNs) and long short-term memory (LSTM) networks for price prediction

In recent years, deep learning models such as recurrent neural networks (RNNs) and long short-term memory (LSTM) networks have shown great promise in predicting cryptocurrency prices. These models are particularly effective for time series analysis, where the model is trained to predict the next value in a sequence based on past values.

One of the key advantages of using RNNs and LSTMs is their ability to capture temporal dependencies in the data. This means that the model can take into account patterns and trends that occur over time, which can be crucial in predicting future prices in a highly volatile market like cryptocurrencies.

RNNs and LSTMs are both types of neural networks that are specifically designed for time series analysis. The basic architecture of an RNN consists of a simple neural network with feedback loops, which allow the model to use information from previous time steps in its predictions. LSTMs, on the other hand, are a type of RNN that are designed to overcome some of the limitations of traditional RNNs, such as the problem of vanishing gradients.

To use RNNs and LSTMs for cryptocurrency price prediction, historical price data is typically used as the input to the model, with the target being the next price value in the sequence. The model is then trained using a technique called backpropagation through time, which involves adjusting the weights of the network to minimize the error between the predicted values and the actual values.

One of the challenges of using deep learning models for price prediction is the potential for overfitting. This occurs when the model becomes too complex and starts to fit the noise in the data, rather than the underlying patterns. To address this, techniques such as regularization and early stopping can be used to prevent the model from becoming too complex.

Despite the challenges, RNNs and LSTMs have shown great promise in predicting cryptocurrency prices. In fact, several research studies have shown that these models can outperform traditional statistical models such as ARIMA and GARCH. However, it's important to note that these models are not perfect and should be used as one tool among many in a comprehensive trading strategy.

Challenges and limitations of predictive modeling for crypto investing

Predictive modeling has been a popular approach in the cryptocurrency market for quite some time, as it allows investors to make informed decisions about future price movements. However, like any other investment strategy, there are challenges and limitations associated with predictive modeling for crypto investing.

One major challenge with predictive modeling is the accuracy of the models themselves. While machine learning algorithms can be trained on large amounts of data, they can still make mistakes when predicting the future. This is because cryptocurrency prices are influenced by a wide variety of factors, some of which are difficult to predict or quantify.

Another challenge with predictive modeling for crypto investing is the speed at which prices can change. Cryptocurrency prices can be highly volatile, and even small fluctuations in price can have a significant impact on an investor's return. This means that predictive models need to be able to respond quickly to changes in the market in order to be effective.

In addition, there are limitations to the amount of data that can be used to train predictive models. While there is a vast amount of historical price data available for most cryptocurrencies, this data may not be enough to accurately predict future price movements. This is because cryptocurrency markets are relatively new and constantly evolving, and past trends may not be indicative of future performance.

Finally, there are also challenges associated with data quality and availability. Cryptocurrency markets are decentralized and largely unregulated, which means that data can be difficult to collect and verify. This can lead to inconsistencies in the data, which can in turn affect the accuracy of predictive models.

Despite these challenges and limitations, predictive modeling remains a powerful tool for crypto investors. By carefully developing and refining predictive models, investors can gain valuable insights into the cryptocurrency market and make informed decisions about when to buy, sell, or hold their investments. However, it is important to approach predictive modeling with caution and to recognize its limitations in order to make the most effective use of this strategy.

Chapter 4: Risk Management and Portfolio Optimization

The importance of risk management in crypto investing

In any type of investing, managing risk is a crucial aspect that can determine the success or failure of an investor. This is particularly true for the volatile and rapidly-changing world of cryptocurrency investing. In recent years, there have been many high-profile cases of investors losing significant amounts of money due to a lack of risk management.

One of the main reasons why risk management is so important in crypto investing is the high level of volatility. The prices of cryptocurrencies can fluctuate rapidly and unpredictably, making it difficult to predict future price movements. This means that even if an investor has a solid trading strategy, there is still a significant risk of losing money if proper risk management techniques are not employed.

One of the key risk management techniques used in crypto investing is diversification. This involves spreading investments across different cryptocurrencies, as well as other asset classes such as stocks, bonds, and commodities. By diversifying, investors can reduce their exposure to any single asset and minimize the impact of any losses. Diversification can be achieved through a variety of means, including investing in different cryptocurrencies with different risk profiles, investing in exchange-traded funds (ETFs), or investing in a managed cryptocurrency fund.

Another important risk management technique is setting stop-loss orders. This involves placing an order with a broker or exchange to automatically sell a cryptocurrency if its price falls below a certain threshold. This can help limit potential losses and reduce the impact of market volatility.

In addition to risk management, portfolio optimization is another important aspect of successful crypto investing. Portfolio optimization involves selecting the right mix of assets to maximize returns while minimizing risk. This can be achieved through various techniques such as modern portfolio theory (MPT) and mean-variance optimization.

MPT is a mathematical framework for constructing portfolios that maximizes expected return for a given level of risk, or minimizes risk for a given level of expected return. This involves selecting assets with low or negative correlation, as this can help reduce overall portfolio risk.

Mean-variance optimization is another technique that can be used to optimize a portfolio. This involves finding the combination of assets that minimizes the variance of the portfolio while achieving a target level of return. This can be achieved through a variety of means, including diversification, asset allocation, and risk management.

In conclusion, risk management and portfolio optimization are crucial aspects of successful crypto investing. By employing proper risk management techniques such as diversification and stop-loss orders, investors can reduce their exposure to market volatility and minimize potential losses. Similarly, by using techniques such as modern portfolio theory and mean-variance optimization, investors can optimize their portfolios to maximize returns while minimizing risk.

How to use AI to optimize portfolio allocations and manage risk

Portfolio optimization is the process of constructing a portfolio of assets that maximizes returns while minimizing risks. In the context of cryptocurrency investing, portfolio optimization is crucial for achieving long-term profitability and stability. One of the challenges of portfolio optimization in the cryptocurrency market is the high volatility of prices, which can lead to large fluctuations in portfolio values. However, AI techniques can be used to manage these risks and optimize portfolio allocations.

One way to use AI for portfolio optimization is to employ a machine learning algorithm to learn the relationships between different cryptocurrencies and their historical price movements. This can be achieved by training the algorithm on a historical dataset of cryptocurrency prices and using it to predict future price movements. The algorithm can then be used to optimize portfolio allocations based on the predicted price movements.

Another approach to portfolio optimization is to use reinforcement learning, where an agent is trained to learn an optimal portfolio allocation strategy through trial and error. The agent's objective is to maximize returns while minimizing risks, and it is rewarded for making profitable trades and penalized for making losses. Through this process, the agent learns to adjust its portfolio allocations based on market conditions and can adapt to changing market conditions over time.

In addition to using AI for portfolio optimization, risk management is also crucial for long-term profitability in cryptocurrency investing. This involves identifying and managing risks associated with cryptocurrency investments, such as market volatility, liquidity risks, and regulatory risks. One way to manage these risks is to employ a diversified investment strategy, which involves investing in a range of different cryptocurrencies and spreading investments across different markets and asset classes.

AI can also be used to manage risk in cryptocurrency investing. For example, machine learning algorithms can be used to identify patterns in market data that signal potential risks, such as sudden price drops or abnormal trading volumes. The algorithm can then be used to trigger risk management strategies, such as selling off certain assets or adjusting portfolio allocations to reduce exposure to risk.

Overall, using AI for portfolio optimization and risk management in cryptocurrency investing can help investors achieve long-term profitability and stability in an increasingly volatile market. However, it is important to recognize that AI techniques are not a silver bullet solution and must be used in conjunction with traditional investment strategies and risk management techniques to achieve optimal results.

Using value at risk (VaR) and other risk metrics to measure and manage portfolio risk

Value at Risk (VaR) is a widely used risk management metric in finance and investment management. It provides an estimate of the potential loss that a portfolio could incur in a specified period of time at a given level of confidence. VaR is a statistical measure of risk that considers the volatility of the portfolio, historical performance, and the level of confidence desired.

In crypto investing, VaR can be a useful tool for measuring portfolio risk and informing investment decisions. As with other assets, cryptocurrencies can be subject to price volatility, market shocks, and other risks. VaR can help investors quantify these risks and make more informed decisions about portfolio allocation and risk management.

To calculate VaR for a crypto portfolio, investors can use historical data to estimate the volatility of the portfolio, then calculate the potential loss at a given level of confidence. For example, an investor may set a VaR of 5% for a portfolio, meaning that they are 95% confident that the portfolio will not lose more than the estimated VaR in a given period of time.

There are several methods for calculating VaR, including historical simulation, variance-covariance, and Monte Carlo simulation. Each method has its advantages and disadvantages, and the choice of method may depend on the specific characteristics of the portfolio and the level of accuracy desired.

Another risk management metric that can be used in conjunction with VaR is conditional value at risk (CVaR), also known as expected shortfall. CVaR measures the expected loss in the tail of the distribution beyond the VaR level. It provides a more complete picture of the potential losses in the worst-case scenarios and can be particularly useful for managing extreme risks.

In addition to VaR and CVaR, there are other risk metrics that can be used in crypto investing, such as maximum drawdown, which measures the maximum loss from peak to trough in a portfolio, and Sharpe ratio, which measures the risk-adjusted return of a portfolio. By using a combination of these metrics, investors can gain a more comprehensive understanding of portfolio risk and make more informed investment decisions.

AI can also be used to optimize portfolio allocations and manage risk by identifying patterns in market data and making predictions about future performance. Machine learning algorithms can analyze historical data to identify correlations between different assets and predict future price movements. These predictions can be used to inform portfolio allocation decisions and manage risk by adjusting allocations based on expected performance.

In addition, AI can be used to automate risk management tasks, such as rebalancing portfolios and setting stop-loss orders. By using AI-powered trading bots, investors can take advantage of market opportunities while minimizing risk and avoiding emotional decision-making.

Overall, the use of VaR and other risk metrics, combined with AI-powered portfolio optimization and risk management, can help investors make more informed investment decisions and manage risk in the volatile and fast-paced world of crypto investing.

How to incorporate alternative data sources into risk management and portfolio optimization strategies

The field of finance has seen a significant increase in the use of alternative data sources over the last decade. Alternative data refers to any data set that is not traditionally used by market participants in their investment decision-making process. These sources can provide valuable insights into market behavior and trends that can be used to inform risk management and portfolio optimization strategies. This chapter will discuss how alternative data sources can be incorporated into risk management and portfolio optimization strategies for cryptocurrency investments.

Alternative Data Sources for Risk Management and Portfolio Optimization:

The use of alternative data sources in risk management and portfolio optimization strategies has become increasingly popular due to the vast amounts of data available through sources such as social media, news articles, and web traffic. Incorporating alternative data sources into these strategies allows investors to gain insights into market behavior that traditional data sources may not capture.

For example, sentiment analysis of social media data can provide insights into investor sentiment and help identify potential market trends. Additionally, web traffic data can provide insights into the popularity of certain cryptocurrencies and their potential for growth. These alternative data sources can be incorporated into risk management and portfolio optimization strategies to inform investment decisions and manage portfolio risk.

Risk Metrics and Alternative Data:

Incorporating alternative data sources into risk management strategies can also help investors develop more accurate risk metrics. Value at risk (VaR) is a widely used metric for measuring portfolio risk. VaR calculates the potential losses that a portfolio could incur over a given time period with a certain level of confidence.

By incorporating alternative data sources, investors can develop more accurate VaR calculations. For example, incorporating sentiment analysis of social media data can help identify potential market trends and adjust VaR calculations accordingly. This can help investors better understand the potential risks associated with their portfolio and adjust their risk management strategies accordingly.

Portfolio Optimization and Alternative Data:

Alternative data sources can also be used to optimize portfolio allocations. By incorporating alternative data sources such as sentiment analysis and web traffic data, investors can gain insights into market behavior and identify potential growth opportunities. This can help inform portfolio allocation decisions and optimize portfolio performance.

For example, sentiment analysis of social media data can help identify cryptocurrencies that are currently popular among investors and have the potential for growth. Additionally, web traffic data can provide insights into the popularity of certain cryptocurrencies and their potential for growth. By incorporating these alternative data sources into portfolio optimization strategies, investors can optimize their portfolio allocations and potentially increase their returns.

Conclusion:

Incorporating alternative data sources into risk management and portfolio optimization strategies can provide valuable insights into market behavior and trends that traditional data sources may not capture. By incorporating sentiment analysis, web traffic data, and other alternative data sources, investors can better manage portfolio risk, develop more accurate risk metrics, and optimize portfolio allocations. As the use of alternative data sources continues to grow, it will become increasingly important for investors to incorporate these sources into their investment decision-making process to stay ahead of the curve in the cryptocurrency market.

Chapter 5: Applying AI to Cryptocurrency Mining

An overview of cryptocurrency mining and how it works

Cryptocurrency mining is the process of validating transactions on a blockchain network and adding new blocks to the blockchain. Miners use specialized hardware and software to solve complex mathematical equations and compete with each other to find the solution first. The first miner to find the solution is rewarded with newly created cryptocurrency as well as transaction fees.

Cryptocurrency mining is a critical component of the blockchain network's security and functionality. Without miners, blockchain networks would not be able to validate transactions, and the network would be vulnerable to attacks.

Cryptocurrency mining was initially designed to be done on regular computers, but as the number of miners grew, the difficulty of the mathematical equations also increased, making it necessary for miners to use specialized hardware. The most commonly used hardware for cryptocurrency mining is the Application-Specific Integrated Circuit (ASIC), which is designed specifically for mining cryptocurrencies.

The mining process can vary depending on the blockchain network being used. Bitcoin, for example, uses the Proof of Work (PoW) consensus mechanism, which requires miners to solve a complex mathematical equation to add new blocks to the blockchain. Ethereum, on the other hand, currently uses a PoW mechanism but is planning to transition to a Proof of Stake (PoS) mechanism in the future.

Mining can be a profitable venture, but it is also very competitive, and the cost of equipment and electricity can be high. In addition, the profitability of mining can be impacted by several factors, such as the price of the cryptocurrency being mined, the difficulty of the equations being solved, and the cost of electricity.

One of the challenges of cryptocurrency mining is that the difficulty of the equations being solved can increase over time, making it more challenging and expensive for miners to stay profitable. This has led to the development of mining pools, where miners combine their resources to increase their chances of solving equations and earning rewards.

Overall, cryptocurrency mining is a critical component of the blockchain ecosystem, and it is essential for miners to stay up-to-date on the latest hardware and software developments to stay competitive and profitable.

How AI is being used to optimize mining operations and improve mining efficiency

Cryptocurrency mining requires significant computational power to solve complex mathematical problems and validate transactions on the blockchain network. As the difficulty of mining increases, miners are constantly seeking ways to optimize their operations and increase their profitability. This is where AI can play a significant role in helping miners improve their efficiency and reduce costs.

Here are some of the ways AI is being used to optimize mining operations:

1. Predictive maintenance: Mining hardware is subjected to heavy usage and is prone to breakdowns. AI-based predictive maintenance models can monitor the performance of mining equipment in real-time and predict when maintenance is required. This allows miners to proactively replace or repair faulty components before they fail, reducing downtime and increasing efficiency.

2. Power optimization: Power is one of the biggest expenses for cryptocurrency miners. AI-based algorithms can analyze data from sensors and meters to optimize power usage and reduce energy consumption. For example, miners can use AI to determine the optimal power levels for their

hardware based on factors such as temperature, humidity, and mining difficulty.

3. Resource allocation: Mining farms often have hundreds or even thousands of mining rigs that need to be managed. AI can help optimize resource allocation by identifying which rigs are performing well and which ones need to be adjusted. This can help miners maximize their hashrate and minimize the amount of wasted computational power.

4. Pool selection: Cryptocurrency miners can choose to join mining pools, which are groups of miners that work together to solve blocks and share the rewards. AI can help miners select the best pool based on factors such as payout structure, fee structure, and hashrate distribution. This can help miners maximize their earnings and reduce their risks.

5. Real-time monitoring: Mining operations generate vast amounts of data, including hashrate, temperature, power consumption, and more. AI-based monitoring systems can process this data in real-time and provide insights that can help miners optimize their operations. For example, miners can use AI to detect when a rig is overheating or when a component is failing, allowing them to take corrective action before a major problem occurs.

6. Market analysis: Cryptocurrency mining profitability is heavily dependent on the market value of the cryptocurrency being mined. AI can analyze market data and provide insights on market trends, price movements, and other factors that can impact mining profitability. This can help miners make informed decisions on which cryptocurrencies to mine and when to sell their holdings.

In conclusion, AI has the potential to revolutionize the cryptocurrency mining industry by improving efficiency, reducing costs, and increasing profitability. As mining becomes increasingly competitive and challenging, miners who adopt AI-based solutions will have a significant advantage over their competitors.

Challenges and limitations of AI in cryptocurrency mining

Cryptocurrency mining is a complex and resource-intensive process that has been the focus of innovation and experimentation in the use of artificial intelligence (AI) to improve efficiency and profitability. While there are potential benefits to using AI in mining, there are also significant challenges and limitations that need to be considered.

One of the primary challenges of using AI in cryptocurrency mining is the complexity of the mining process. Mining requires specialized hardware and software that can perform complex calculations to verify transactions and create new blocks in the blockchain. This process involves many variables and can be affected by external factors such as changes in network difficulty, fluctuations in cryptocurrency prices, and changes in mining rewards. Developing AI systems that can effectively analyze and respond to these variables is a significant challenge.

Another challenge of using AI in cryptocurrency mining is the high energy consumption associated with mining. Mining operations require large amounts of electricity to power the hardware used for mining, which can lead to high energy costs and environmental concerns. While there have been attempts to use AI to optimize energy usage in mining, these efforts are still in the early stages of development and implementation.

Additionally, the use of AI in mining is limited by the availability of data. Mining operations generate large amounts of data, but this data can be difficult to access and analyze effectively. Furthermore, there are privacy concerns associated with mining data, which can limit the availability of data for AI training and analysis.

Despite these challenges, there are also potential benefits to using AI in cryptocurrency mining. One of the primary benefits is the potential for increased efficiency and profitability. AI can be used to optimize mining operations, reduce energy usage, and improve the accuracy of mining calculations. This can result in increased mining rewards and reduced costs, leading to higher profitability for mining operations.

Another benefit of using AI in cryptocurrency mining is the potential for improved security. Mining is an essential component of the blockchain's security model, as it provides a means of verifying transactions and creating new blocks. By using AI to improve the efficiency and accuracy of mining operations, mining can become more secure, making it more challenging for bad actors to compromise the blockchain.

In conclusion, while there are significant challenges and limitations to using AI in cryptocurrency mining, there are also potential benefits. As the technology continues to develop and evolve, it is likely that we will see more innovative and effective uses of AI in mining operations. However, it is important to approach these developments with a critical eye and consider the potential risks and limitations associated with the use of AI in mining.

Chapter 6: Building Your Own AI-Driven Crypto Trading System

A step-by-step guide to building your own AI-driven crypto trading system

Building your own AI-driven crypto trading system may seem daunting, but with the right tools and guidance, it can be a rewarding and profitable venture. In this guide, we'll provide a step-by-step overview of the process of building your own trading system using artificial intelligence.

Step 1: Define your trading strategy The first step in building an AI-driven trading system is to define your trading strategy. This involves determining your goals, risk tolerance, and preferred trading style. Your strategy should be based on sound investment principles and be adaptable to changing market conditions.

Step 2: Collect and analyze data The next step is to collect and analyze data to inform your trading strategy. This data can come from a variety of sources, including market data, news and social media sentiment analysis, and alternative data sources like blockchain transaction data. Machine learning algorithms can be used to analyze this data and identify patterns and trends that can inform your trading decisions.

Step 3: Choose the right AI tools To build your AI-driven trading system, you'll need to choose the right tools and technologies. There are a variety of open-source and commercial AI frameworks and libraries available, such as TensorFlow, PyTorch, and scikit-learn. You'll also need to select the appropriate hardware and cloud infrastructure to support your system.

Step 4: Train your AI model Once you have your data and tools in place, you can begin training your AI model. This involves feeding historical data into your model and using machine learning algorithms to teach it to make predictions about future market movements. You'll need to fine-tune your model over time to improve its accuracy and performance.

Step 5: Test and refine your system After you've trained your model, it's time to test and refine your trading system. You can do this by running simulations and backtesting your system using historical data. This will help you identify any weaknesses or areas for improvement in your system and make adjustments accordingly.

Step 6: Deploy your system Once you're satisfied with the performance of your trading system, it's time to deploy it in the real world. This involves integrating your AI model into a trading platform or exchange and setting up automated trading rules based on your strategy. You'll also need to monitor your system's performance over time and make adjustments as needed.

Challenges and considerations Building an AI-driven crypto trading system is a complex process that requires a deep understanding of both finance and machine learning. There are several challenges and considerations to keep in mind when embarking on this venture.

First, it's important to remember that no trading system is foolproof, and even the best AI models can make mistakes or be susceptible to unexpected market events. It's essential to have a risk management plan in place to mitigate potential losses.

Second, data quality is critical to the success of your AI model. Garbage in, garbage out applies to AI just as it does to any other data-driven system. It's essential to ensure that your data is accurate, complete, and up-to-date.

Finally, it's important to stay up-to-date with the latest developments in both the cryptocurrency market and AI technologies. The market is constantly evolving, and new tools and techniques are emerging all the time. By staying informed and adaptable, you can ensure that your trading system remains competitive and profitable over the long term.

Conclusion Building your own AI-driven crypto trading system can be a challenging but rewarding endeavor. By following the steps outlined in this guide and remaining vigilant to the challenges and considerations, you can develop a profitable trading system that leverages the power of artificial intelligence to outperform the market.

How to choose the right AI tools and technologies for your trading system

Introduction: When building an AI-driven crypto trading system, it's essential to choose the right tools and technologies. In this section, we'll explore some of the critical factors to consider when selecting the appropriate AI tools and technologies for your trading system.

1. Determine your trading strategy: The first step in selecting the right AI tools and technologies for your trading system is to determine your trading strategy. Are you going to use a high-frequency trading strategy, a long-term investment strategy, or something in between? Different trading strategies require different AI tools and technologies. For example, if you're using a high-frequency trading strategy, you'll need a system that can execute trades quickly and handle large volumes of data in real-time.

2. Choose the right machine learning algorithms: The next step is to choose the right machine learning algorithms for your trading system. There are several types of machine learning algorithms, including supervised learning, unsupervised learning, and reinforcement learning. Supervised learning algorithms are used to train models based on historical data, while unsupervised learning algorithms are used to discover patterns in data.

Reinforcement learning algorithms are used to train models to make decisions based on rewards or penalties. Choosing the right machine learning algorithm for your trading system is critical to its success.

3. Consider cloud-based solutions: Another important factor to consider when selecting AI tools and technologies for your trading system is whether to use cloud-based solutions or on-premise solutions. Cloud-based solutions offer several advantages, including scalability, cost-effectiveness, and easy access to data. Additionally, cloud-based solutions often come with pre-built AI models and tools, making it easier to get started with AI-driven trading.

4. Evaluate the quality of data: Data is the lifeblood of an AI-driven trading system. Therefore, it's crucial to evaluate the quality of data before selecting AI tools and technologies. Quality data includes clean, reliable, and accurate data that's relevant to your trading strategy. Ensure that you have access to historical data, real-time data, and alternative data sources to ensure that your trading system can make informed decisions.

5. Look for user-friendly interfaces: User-friendly interfaces are critical when selecting AI tools and technologies for your trading system. Ensure that the tools and technologies you choose have user-friendly interfaces

that are easy to use and understand. Additionally, look for tools that offer visualization and reporting features that make it easy to monitor and analyze your trading performance.

6. Consider the cost: The cost is an essential factor when selecting AI tools and technologies for your trading system. Consider the cost of purchasing, maintaining, and updating the tools and technologies. Additionally, factor in any costs associated with data storage, data processing, and other related expenses.

Conclusion: Selecting the right AI tools and technologies is critical when building an AI-driven crypto trading system. Consider your trading strategy, choose the right machine learning algorithms, evaluate the quality of data, look for user-friendly interfaces, and consider the cost when selecting AI tools and technologies for your trading system. By following these steps, you'll be well on your way to building a successful AI-driven crypto trading system.

Tips and best practices for building and deploying an effective AI-driven trading system

Building and deploying an effective AI-driven crypto trading system can be a complex task that requires knowledge of both AI and trading. In this section, we will provide some tips and best practices that can help you build and deploy an effective AI-driven trading system.

1. Define your trading strategy: Before you start building your trading system, it is important to define your trading strategy. Your trading strategy should outline the types of trades you want to make, the risk management strategies you will use, and your investment goals. Your trading strategy will guide the development of your trading system and help you make informed decisions about what data to use and how to use it.

2. Choose the right data: The quality of the data you use is critical to the success of your trading system. You should use a variety of data sources, including price data, volume data, news data, and social media data. Make sure the data you use is accurate, up-to-date, and relevant to your trading strategy.

3. Use the right AI tools: There are many AI tools and technologies available for building trading systems. You should choose tools that are best suited for your needs and

your level of expertise. Some popular AI tools for trading include Python, TensorFlow, Keras, and scikit-learn.

4. Build a robust backtesting system: Backtesting is the process of testing your trading strategy using historical data to see how it would have performed in the past. A robust backtesting system is essential for evaluating the performance of your trading system and making improvements. Make sure your backtesting system includes realistic transaction costs, slippage, and other factors that can affect your trading results.

5. Monitor and refine your trading system: Once your trading system is up and running, it is important to monitor its performance and make adjustments as needed. Keep track of your trading results and use them to identify areas where your trading system can be improved. You may need to make changes to your trading strategy, data sources, or AI tools to optimize the performance of your trading system.

6. Follow best practices for deployment: When deploying your trading system, it is important to follow best practices to ensure its stability and reliability. This includes using version control to manage your code, implementing proper error handling and logging, and testing your trading system in a controlled environment before deploying it to production.

7. Stay up-to-date with the latest AI and trading trends: The AI and trading landscapes are constantly evolving, so it is important to stay up-to-date with the latest trends and developments. Attend conferences and webinars, read industry blogs and publications, and participate in online communities to stay informed about the latest AI and trading technologies and best practices.

In summary, building and deploying an effective AI-driven trading system requires careful planning, the right data, the right AI tools, a robust backtesting system, monitoring and refinement, best practices for deployment, and staying up-to-date with the latest trends and developments. By following these tips and best practices, you can build a trading system that can help you make informed trading decisions and achieve your investment goals.

Conclusion

Recap of the key insights and takeaways from the book

The field of cryptocurrency investing and trading is rapidly evolving, and the emergence of AI-driven approaches has created new opportunities for investors and traders to achieve superior results. Throughout this book, we have explored the various ways in which AI can be used to improve cryptocurrency investing and trading, including using machine learning and predictive modeling techniques to predict price movements, applying risk management strategies to manage portfolio risk, and using AI to optimize mining operations.

In this chapter, we will provide a recap of the key insights and takeaways from the book.

Firstly, we highlighted the importance of understanding the fundamentals of the cryptocurrency market before diving into AI-driven approaches. It is essential to have a deep understanding of the market's dynamics and drivers, including the technical aspects of cryptocurrencies, such as mining, blockchain technology, and consensus algorithms, as well as the broader economic and regulatory landscape.

We then explored the various ways in which AI can be used to improve cryptocurrency investing and trading. One key insight was that AI is particularly effective in identifying patterns and predicting price movements. Techniques such as machine learning and predictive modeling can be used to analyze vast amounts of data and identify patterns that may not be immediately apparent to human analysts.

Another key takeaway was the importance of risk management in cryptocurrency investing and trading. AI-driven approaches can help to identify potential risks and mitigate them before they become significant problems. Risk management strategies, such as diversification and the use of value at risk (VaR) metrics, can be applied to optimize portfolio allocations and minimize downside risk.

We also discussed how AI can be used to optimize cryptocurrency mining operations. AI-driven approaches can help to improve mining efficiency and reduce energy consumption, thereby reducing costs and increasing profitability.

Finally, we provided a step-by-step guide to building your own AI-driven crypto trading system, including tips and best practices for choosing the right AI tools and technologies and deploying an effective trading system.

Overall, this book has demonstrated the significant potential for AI to improve cryptocurrency investing and trading. However, it is essential to approach AI-driven approaches with caution, as there are challenges and limitations to consider, such as data quality, overfitting, and black box models.

In conclusion, the cryptocurrency market is constantly evolving, and the use of AI-driven approaches is likely to become increasingly prevalent in the years ahead. By understanding the fundamentals of the market, using AI-driven approaches to predict price movements and manage risk, and leveraging AI to optimize mining operations and build effective trading systems, investors and traders can gain a significant competitive advantage in this exciting and rapidly growing market.

The future of AI-driven crypto investing and how to stay ahead of the curve

The emergence of AI-driven crypto investing has revolutionized the way investors approach the cryptocurrency market. As AI technologies continue to advance, we can expect to see even more significant changes in the crypto investment landscape. In this section, we will discuss the future of AI-driven crypto investing and provide some tips on how investors can stay ahead of the curve.

The Future of AI-Driven Crypto Investing

One of the most significant advantages of using AI in crypto investing is the ability to quickly analyze vast amounts of data from a variety of sources. As AI technologies continue to improve, we can expect to see even more sophisticated algorithms that can provide even more accurate and reliable predictions. Additionally, the use of AI in the crypto market will likely become more widespread as investors become more comfortable with the technology.

Another potential development in the future of AI-driven crypto investing is the integration of blockchain technology. Blockchain technology provides a secure and transparent way to record and verify transactions, making it an ideal technology for the crypto market. By combining AI and blockchain technology, investors can create even more robust and secure investment strategies.

Finally, we can expect to see an increase in the use of AI-driven trading bots. These bots use sophisticated algorithms to analyze market trends and execute trades automatically, without the need for human intervention. As AI technologies continue to improve, we can expect these bots to become even more advanced, providing investors with even more opportunities to make profitable trades.

Tips for Staying Ahead of the Curve

As the crypto investment landscape continues to evolve, it's important for investors to stay ahead of the curve. Here are a few tips to help you stay ahead of the game:

1. Stay up-to-date on the latest AI technologies: As AI technologies continue to advance, it's important to stay up-to-date on the latest developments. Attend conferences, read industry publications, and network with other investors to stay informed.

2. Experiment with different AI tools and technologies: There is no one-size-fits-all solution when it comes to AI-driven crypto investing. Experiment with different tools and technologies to find the ones that work best for you.

3. Keep an eye on regulatory developments: As the crypto market continues to grow, it's likely that regulators will start to take notice. Keep an eye on regulatory developments and make sure that you are operating within the bounds of the law.

4. Be patient: AI-driven investing is still in its early stages, and it may take some time before we see widespread adoption. Be patient and continue to experiment with different strategies until you find what works best for you.

Conclusion

AI-driven crypto investing has the potential to revolutionize the way we approach the cryptocurrency market. By using sophisticated algorithms to analyze vast amounts of data, investors can make more informed and profitable investment decisions. However, as with any new technology, there are challenges and limitations that must be overcome. By staying up-to-date on the latest AI technologies, experimenting with different tools and technologies, and keeping an eye on regulatory developments, investors can stay ahead of the curve and capitalize on the many opportunities that AI-driven crypto investing has to offer.

Advice for readers who are interested in exploring AI-driven crypto investing further

As we have seen throughout this book, the world of cryptocurrency investing is evolving rapidly, and artificial intelligence is playing an increasingly important role in this space. In this final chapter, we will provide advice for readers who are interested in exploring AI-driven crypto investing further.

Advice for Exploring AI-Driven Crypto Investing:

1. Keep Learning: One of the most important pieces of advice we can give is to keep learning. The field of AI and cryptocurrency investing is rapidly evolving, and staying up-to-date with the latest trends and technologies is critical. Attend conferences, read research papers, and follow thought leaders on social media to stay informed.

2. Build a Strong Foundation: Before diving into AI-driven crypto investing, it is important to have a strong foundation in traditional investing principles. This includes understanding risk management, portfolio optimization, and market analysis.

3. Choose the Right AI Tools and Technologies: As we discussed earlier in the book, there are a wide variety of AI tools and technologies available for crypto investing. Choose the ones that align with your investing strategy and goals.

Consider factors such as the ease of use, the level of customization, and the level of technical expertise required.

4. Test Your Strategies: Before deploying your AI-driven trading system in the real world, it is important to test your strategies thoroughly. This can be done using historical data or in a simulated trading environment.

5. Don't Over-Rely on AI: While AI can be a powerful tool for investing, it is important not to over-rely on it. AI-driven trading systems should be used in conjunction with traditional investing principles, and human oversight is still critical.

6. Be Patient: AI-driven investing is not a get-rich-quick scheme. It requires patience, discipline, and a long-term perspective. Don't be swayed by short-term market fluctuations, and stick to your investing strategy.

7. Work with Professionals: If you are new to AI-driven crypto investing or feel overwhelmed by the complexity of the field, consider working with professionals. This can include financial advisors, AI experts, or crypto investing specialists.

Conclusion:

As we have seen throughout this book, AI-driven crypto investing has the potential to revolutionize the way we invest in cryptocurrencies. While there are challenges and limitations to this approach, we believe that the benefits far outweigh the risks. By following the advice provided in this chapter, readers can position themselves to take advantage of the opportunities presented by AI-driven crypto investing and stay ahead of the curve.

THE END

Glossary

Here are some key terms and definitions related to AI-driven cryptocurrency investing:

1. Artificial Intelligence (AI): A branch of computer science that aims to create intelligent machines that can perform tasks that typically require human intelligence, such as learning, reasoning, and decision-making.

2. Cryptocurrency: A digital or virtual currency that uses cryptography to secure and verify transactions and to control the creation of new units. Cryptocurrencies are decentralized and operate independently of a central bank.

3. Trading strategy: A set of rules or guidelines that a trader uses to make buy and sell decisions in the market. Trading strategies can be based on technical analysis, fundamental analysis, or a combination of both.

4. Predictive modeling: The use of statistical algorithms and machine learning techniques to analyze historical data and make predictions about future events. In the context of cryptocurrency investing, predictive modeling can be used to forecast price movements.

5. Risk management: The process of identifying, assessing, and controlling potential risks that could impact the performance of an investment portfolio. Risk

management strategies aim to minimize losses and maximize returns.

6. Portfolio optimization: The process of selecting the optimal combination of assets to achieve a desired level of return while minimizing risk. Portfolio optimization strategies take into account factors such as diversification, risk tolerance, and investment goals.

7. Cryptocurrency mining: The process of adding new transactions to the blockchain and verifying transactions using specialized hardware and software. Cryptocurrency mining is the process by which new units of a cryptocurrency are created.

8. Deep learning: A subset of machine learning that involves training artificial neural networks to learn from large amounts of data. Deep learning algorithms are used in a wide range of applications, including image and speech recognition, natural language processing, and predictive modeling.

9. Neural networks: A type of machine learning algorithm that is inspired by the structure and function of the human brain. Neural networks consist of interconnected nodes that process and transmit information.

10. Long short-term memory (LSTM): A type of recurrent neural network (RNN) that is particularly well-

suited for processing sequential data, such as time series. LSTMs are capable of capturing long-term dependencies and are often used in natural language processing and speech recognition.

11. Value at risk (VaR): A risk metric that measures the potential loss of an investment portfolio over a given time period, taking into account the probability of different levels of loss. VaR is a popular metric used in risk management strategies.

12. Alternative data sources: Data sources that are not traditionally used in financial analysis but can provide valuable insights into market trends and consumer behavior. Examples of alternative data sources include social media activity, satellite imagery, and web traffic data.

Potential References

Introduction:

- Narayanan, A., & Narayanan, V. (2019). Cryptocurrencies and blockchain technology. Communications of the ACM, 62(11), 76-84.

Chapter 1: Algorithmic Trading Strategies

- Chan, E. P., & Lai, K. K. (2019). Algorithmic trading: A review of its strengths and weaknesses. Pacific-Basin Finance Journal, 57, 101197.

- Zohar, A., Adam, J. K., & Koppel, M. (2020). Application of algorithmic trading strategies in bitcoin. Journal of Risk and Financial Management, 13(7), 150.

- Arun, P., Singh, V., & Gupta, M. (2018). A comprehensive study on algorithmic trading. Journal of Computer Science and Applications, 6(2), 20-24.

Chapter 2: Reinforcement Learning for Crypto Investing

- Sutton, R. S., & Barto, A. G. (2018). Reinforcement learning: An introduction. MIT Press.

- Liu, Y., Chen, H., & Chen, X. (2021). Applying reinforcement learning to cryptocurrency trading. Journal of Intelligent & Fuzzy Systems, 41(1), 1007-1018.

- Jiang, X., Zhang, Z., & Li, D. (2018). Deep reinforcement learning for automated stock trading: An ensemble strategy. Neurocomputing, 275, 1224-1233.

Chapter 3: Predictive Modeling for Cryptocurrency Prices
- Taylor, M. P., & Sarno, L. (2018). The economics of exchange rates. Cambridge University Press.
- Han, X., Wang, X., & Yu, F. (2019). Bitcoin price forecasting with deep learning: A comparative study. Journal of Risk and Financial Management, 12(4), 177.
- Guo, Y., & Li, X. (2019). Bitcoin price prediction using machine learning: An approach to sample dimension engineering. Journal of Risk and Financial Management, 12(1), 9.

Chapter 4: Risk Management and Portfolio Optimization
- Alexander, C. (2017). Market risk analysis, value at risk models. Wiley.
- Tang, J., Liu, Z., & He, X. (2021). Portfolio optimization of cryptocurrencies using CVaR model. Applied Soft Computing, 99, 106921.
- Bouri, E., Shahzad, S. J. H., Raza, N., & Roubaud, D. (2020). Cryptocurrency portfolio management with downside risk evaluation. Journal of Risk and Financial Management, 13(2), 20.

Chapter 5: Applying AI to Cryptocurrency Mining
- Antonopoulos, A. M. (2014). Mastering Bitcoin: Unlocking Digital Cryptocurrencies. O'Reilly Media, Inc.

- Hoang, D. T., Vu, H. T., & Nguyen, T. H. (2021). An intelligent system for predicting cryptocurrency mining profitability. Journal of Cleaner Production, 292, 126111.

- Su, J., He, P., Wang, Y., & Liu, J. (2018). A novel cryptocurrency mining malware detection method based on behavior analysis. Future Generation Computer Systems, 82, 1-9.

Chapter 6: Building Your Own AI-Driven Crypto Trading System

Chollet, F. (2018). Deep learning with Python. Manning Publications.

Goodfellow, I., Bengio, Y., & Courville, A. (2016). Deep learning. MIT press.

Kingma, D. P., & Ba, J. (2014). Adam: A method for stochastic optimization. arXiv preprint arXiv:1412.6980.

Ranganath, R., Tran, D., & Blei, D. M. (2014). Hierarchical variational models. arXiv preprint arXiv:1409.1556.

Singh, J. P., & Srivastava, G. (2019). Machine learning and blockchain: a powerful combination for supply chain management. Journal of Enterprise Information Management, 32(2), 305-324.

Sutton, R. S., & Barto, A. G. (2018). Reinforcement learning: An introduction. MIT press.

Conclusion

Deng, Y., Bao, F., Kong, Y., Ren, Z., & Dai, Q. (2019). Deep learning for sentiment analysis: A survey. Wiley Interdisciplinary Reviews: Data Mining and Knowledge Discovery, 9(4), e1333.

Glaser, F., & Zimmermann, K. (2018). Beyond bitcoin – a critical look at blockchain-based systems. In International Conference on Business Information Systems (pp. 281-293). Springer, Cham.

Goodfellow, I., Bengio, Y., & Courville, A. (2016). Deep learning. MIT press.

Kshetri, N. (2018). Blockchain's roles in meeting key supply chain management objectives. International Journal of Information Management, 39, 80-89.

LeCun, Y., Bengio, Y., & Hinton, G. (2015). Deep learning. Nature, 521(7553), 436-444.

Sutton, R. S., & Barto, A. G. (2018). Reinforcement learning: An introduction. MIT press.

www.ingramcontent.com/pod-product-compliance
Lightning Source LLC
LaVergne TN
LVHW012126070526
838202LV00056B/5872